Surprise Guests

BY MIIKO SHAFFIER
co-written by Chana Grosser

Illustrated by: Dmitry Gitelman (diemgi.com)
Layout & Design by: Ken Parker (visual-variables.com)

Published by:
Shefer Publishing
www.SheferPublishing.com

For permissions, comments and ordering information write:
Miiko@LearnHebrew.tv

ISBN 978-1-958999-02-8

SURPRISE GUESTS

an **EASY EEVREET STORY**

BY MIIKO SHAFFIER

SHEFER
PUBLISHING

Based on Genesis, Chapter 18, Verses 1-15 and Genesis, Chapter 21, Verse 1.

This story can be read like any English story book. When you get to a Hebrew word, do your best to sound it out and guess the meaning. You can check the pronunciation and meaning in the back of the book.

HAVE FUN!

He loved giving charity and helping others, and he especially loved welcoming guests. In those days, there were no hotels, or hostels. There weren't any trains or cars either. People traveled from one place to another by donkey or camel.

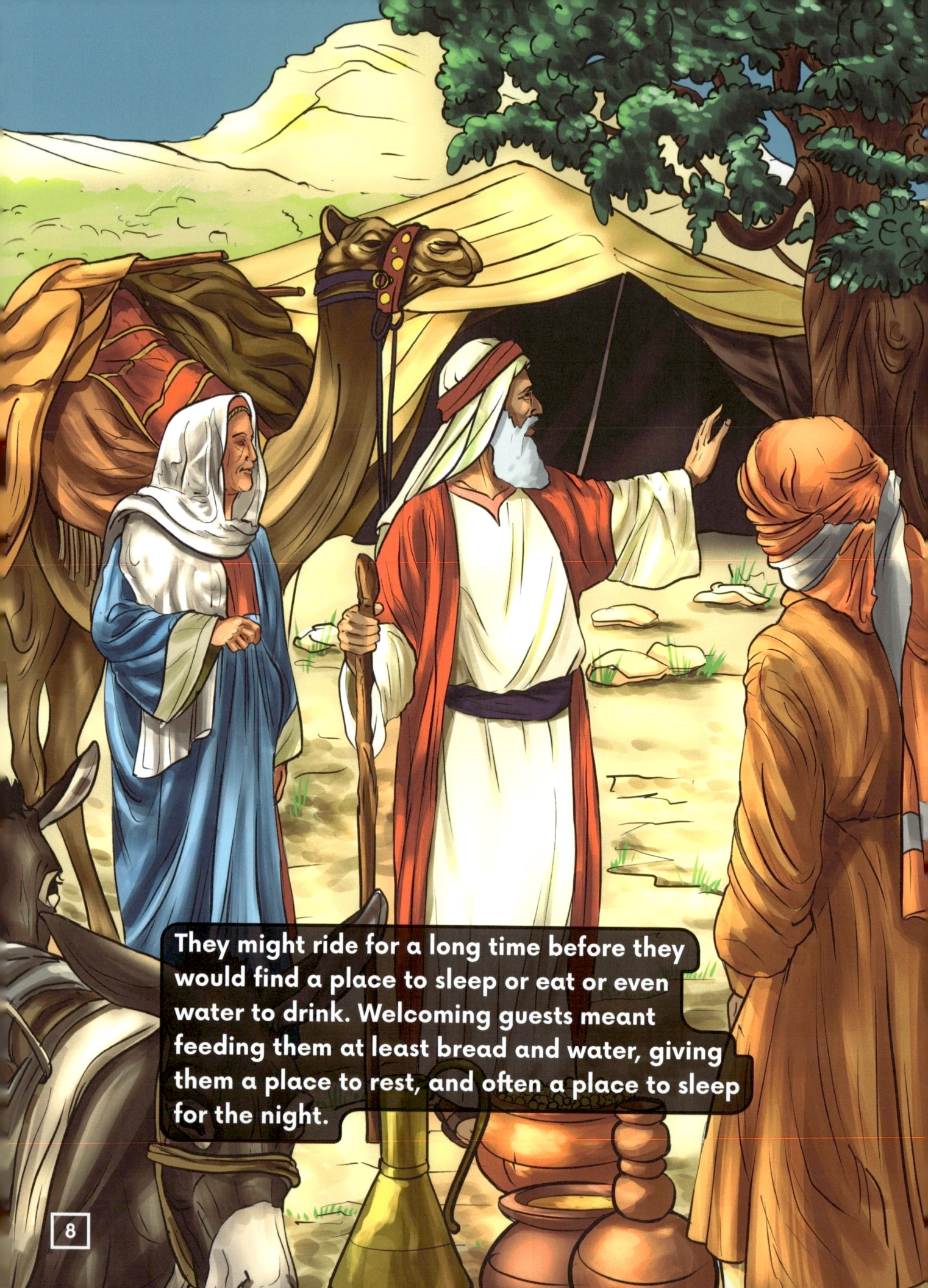

They might ride for a long time before they would find a place to sleep or eat or even water to drink. Welcoming guests meant feeding them at least bread and water, giving them a place to rest, and often a place to sleep for the night.

At the age of ninety-nine אַבְרָהָם was still excited to welcome guests to his אֹהֶל, and his אֹהֶל was always open for visitors.

9

On one very hot day, when the sun was high in the afternoon sky, אַבְרָהָם was waiting in the פֶּתַח of his אֹהֶל.

He squinted in the sun,
Peered across the land.
Beard white,
Skin wrinkled and tanned.
Could there be a traveler near?
Would a caravan of guests appear?

The sun beat strongly on the land. Outside it felt as hot as fire. It wasn't a day travelers would be out. But אַבְרָהָם longed for guests.

G-d saw that אַבְרָהָם was disappointed.

Instead of resting inside the cool אֹהֶל, he was waiting for guests near the פֶּתַח. G-d decided to make אַבְרָהָם happy and send three guests.

אַבְרָהָם stood up abruptly.
Could it be people approaching?
Would he have guests after all?

Three guests were coming! They approached the אֹהֶל slowly. Not sure if they were welcome.

But **אַבְרָהָם** rushed out to meet them: "Come sit in the breeze beneath the **עֵץ**. I'm so pleased to meet you three! You can rest here, wash your feet, I will bring you **מַיִם** to drink and **לֶחֶם** to eat."

The guests saw how happy **אַבְרָהָם** was to host them, and they answered him: "**כֵּן, כֵּן**! We will join you."

אַבְרָהָם felt great. He hurried to his wife who was inside their אֹהֶל to tell her the news.

"SahRahH! SahRahH! An amazing thing has happened. Three guests have arrived! Here is fine flour to make your delicious, round loaves of לֶחֶם."

Then he רָץ to his herd of cows. He chose a calf to be slaughtered for a festive meal for their guests. He asked the shepherd נַעַר to help prepare the calf.

אַבְרָהָם continued his preparations. He took חָלָב and חֶמְאָה and put it with the loaves of לֶחֶם SahRahH had baked. He brought these, together with the prepared meat and served their three guests.

With אַבְרָהָם standing by to serve, the three guests sat in the shade of the עֵץ to enjoy their meal.

19

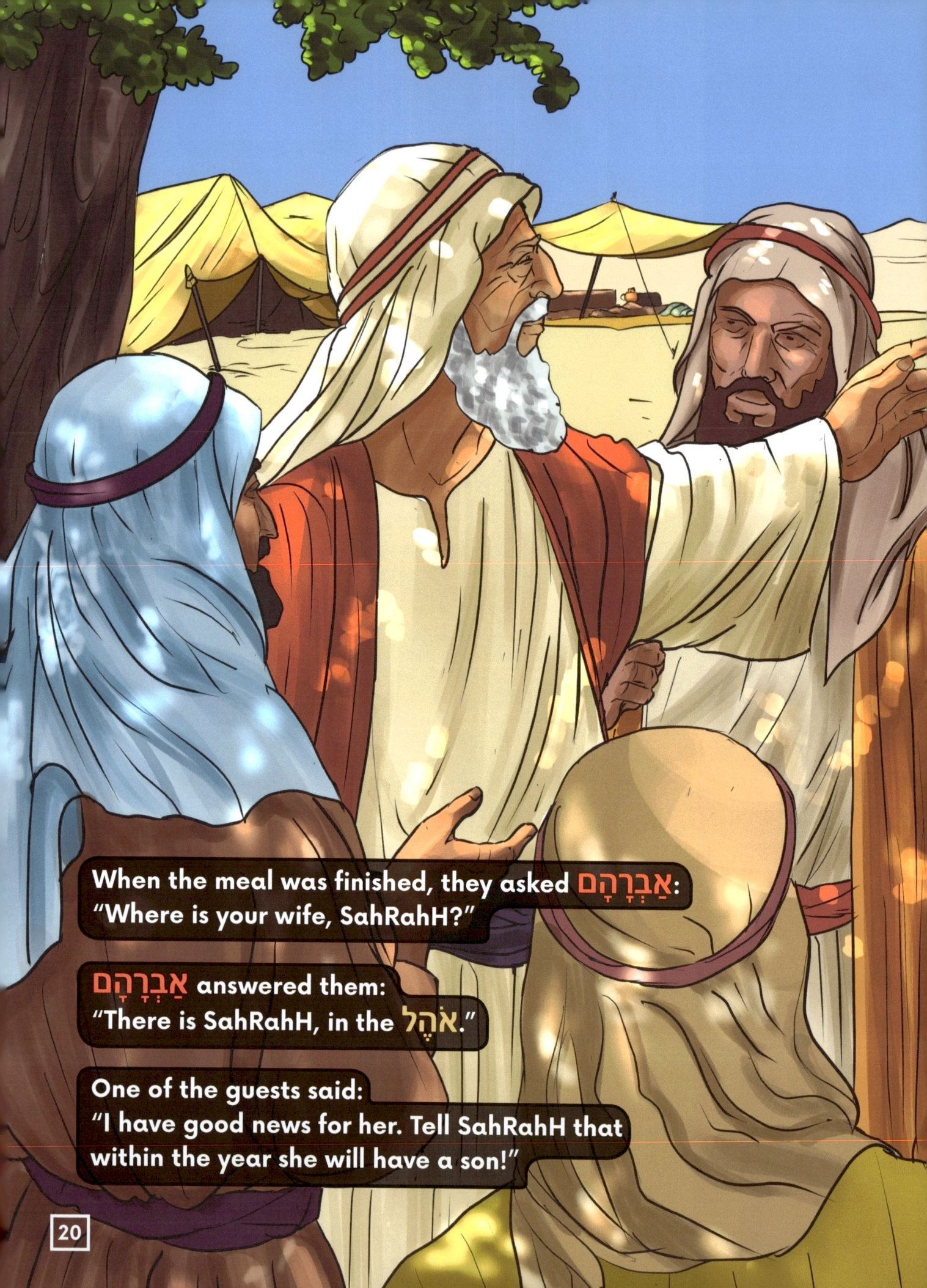

When the meal was finished, they asked אַבְרָהָם:
"Where is your wife, SahRahH?"

אַבְרָהָם answered them:
"There is SahRahH, in the אֹהֶל."

One of the guests said:
"I have good news for her. Tell SahRahH that
within the year she will have a son!"

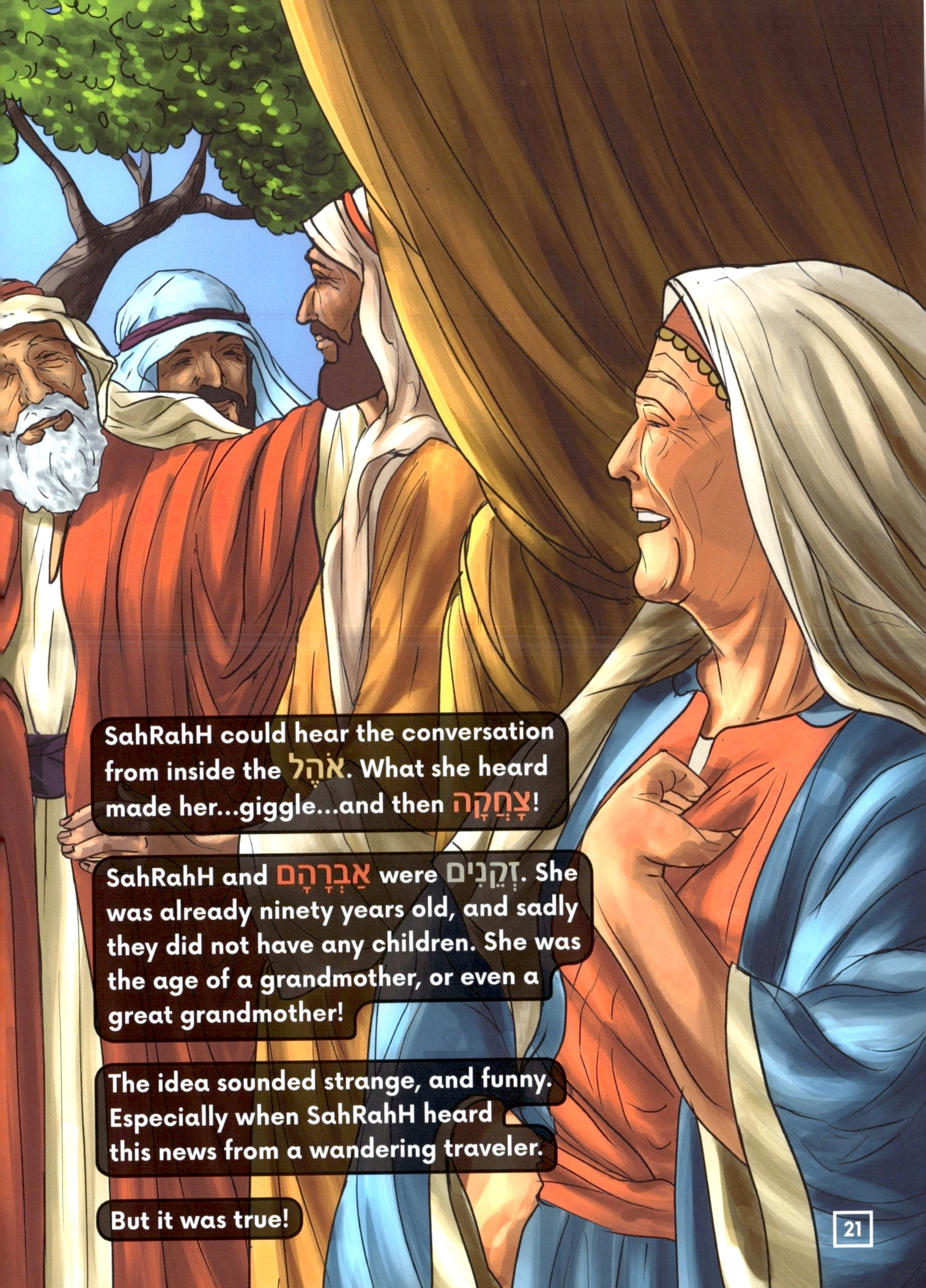

SahRahH could hear the conversation from inside the אֹהֶל. What she heard made her...giggle...and then צָחֲקָה!

SahRahH and אַבְרָהָם were זְקֵנִים. She was already ninety years old, and sadly they did not have any children. She was the age of a grandmother, or even a great grandmother!

The idea sounded strange, and funny. Especially when SahRahH heard this news from a wandering traveler.

But it was true!

אַבְרָהָם was a holy man and G-d would sometimes speak to him. G-d asked אַבְרָהָם: "לָמָה did צָחֲקָה SahRahH לָמָה? she say, "How could I have a baby when I'm so old?"

Just like your guest said, within a year, a son will be born to YOU, אַבְרָהָם and SahRahH!"

What joy! אַבְרָהָם and SahRahH had been waiting for this moment for so many years.

A year later a son was born to אַבְרָהָם and SahRahH. They called their son יִצְחָק. יִצְחָק means "he will laugh." יִצְחָק was named after the great miracle which brought laughter and joy.

24

Here are the Hebrew words from this *Easy Eevreet Story*:

אַבְרָהָם   'ahV-RahHahM | p. 6,9,10-12,14,16, 18-24

the Hebrew name for **ABRAHAM**

אֹהֶל   'ohHehL - **TENT** | p. 9,10,11,13,16, 20,21

פֶּתַח   PehTahCH - **OPENING** | p. 10,11

עֵץ   'ehTZ - **TREE** | p. 14,19

'ehTZ can also mean **WOOD**

מַיִם   MahYeeM - **WATER** | p. 14

לֶחֶם   LehCHehM - **BREAD** | p. 14,16,18

כֵּן   KehN - **YES** | p. 14

...and the opposite is לֹא Loh' - **NO**

רָץ   RahTZ - **HE RAN** | p. 17

נַעַר   Nah'ahR - **YOUTH OR TEENAGER** | p. 17

 CHahLahV - **MILK** | p. 18

 CHehM-'ahH - **BUTTER** | p. 18

 TZahCHahKahH - **SHE LAUGHED** | p. 21,22

If you want to say he laughed, use this word:

צָחַק TZahCHahK - **HE LAUGHED**

זְקֵנִים Z-KehNeeYM - **OLD (PLURAL)** | p. 21

In Hebrew, when you use a word to describe more than one thing or person, the description word (the adjective) needs to be plural too. If you want to describe only one person or thing as being old use this word:

זָקֵן ZahKehN - **OLD**

 LahMahH - **WHY** | p. 22

 YeeTZ-CHahK | p. 24

the Hebrew name for **ISAAC** that literally means (he) will laugh.

You did it! You're learning Hebrew and you can already start to use the words you learned. You can even write up a little list of basics for the grocery store.

חָלָב
חֶמְאָה
מַיִם
לֶחֶם

And you're all set to answer questions with כֵּן or לֹא.

Before you go, here's a bonus question. What do you think the Hebrew word מַצְחִיק - MahTZ-CHeeYK means?

Hint: This word sounds a lot like like the word צָחֲקָה (she laughed) and the name יִצְחָק (he will laugh.) Well since you're used to reading from right to left, here's the answer written from right to left: **YNNUF.**

Hi!

My name is **Miiko.** I live in Be'er Sheva, Israel. My husband Aaron and I have nine kids: Menucha, Mendel, Dovi, Yisroel, Freida, Devora, Fitche, Geula, and Azaria.

I teach Hebrew reading with a fun little book called *Learn to Read Hebrew in 6 Weeks!*

My second book *The Hebrew Workbook* teaches readers to write in Hebrew.

Surprise Guests is part of a series of storybooks that teach Hebrew vocabulary to kids.

I'm so pleased to be a part of your Hebrew journey. If you have any questions or want to say hi please send me an email!
Miiko@LearnHebrew.tv

To the Parents

This book is designed to teach Hebrew vocabulary to people who already know how to read the Hebrew alphabet. While reading this Bible story in English you'll come across Hebrew words embedded in the text. Sound out the words and try to guess their meaning from the context. Check the key in the back of the book to see if you were right.

I've chosen to transliterate the names of the biblical characters mentioned in this story so that you'll learn the authentic Hebrew pronunciation of these biblical names.

Transliteration

Surprise Guests uses the same system of transliteration as my first book *Learn to Read Hebrew in 6 Weeks!*

I came up with a unique transliteration system. It's designed to have the reader pronouncing the Hebrew words accurately without ever having heard a Hebrew speaker pronounce those words.

Here's a breakdown of the system:

Each consonant is represented as a capital letter and each vowel by small letters.

The silent letters 'ahLehF (א) and 'ahYeeN (ע) are represented by an apostrophe (')

The silent vowel 'Sh-Vah' (:) is represented as a hyphen (-).

An important exception to make note of:
The CH does not represent the ch sound like in *chair* or *chest*. In fact, Hebrew doesn't have the ch sound like *chair* or *chest* at all.

The CH represents the letters CHehT(ח) and CHahF(כ) and Final ChahF(ך). These letters make a sound not found in the English language. It's a chokey sound that almost sounds like a kitten purring but much harsher. Think about the name of the composer Bach. From what my Spanish speaking students tell me, it's the same sound as the guttural J in Spanish.

Let's look at the first word in the Hebrew Scripture as an example of how my system works:

בְּרֵאשִׁית

I transliterate it:
B-Reh'SHeeYT

Others may transliterate Bereshit or Bresheet but then you wouldn't know if the vowels are long or short.

If you learned to read Hebrew using my other book, you are already well familiar with this system. But in case you learned to read Hebrew elsewhere, here's a key to make sure it's clear.

א	ב	ב	ג	ד	ה	ו
'	B	V	G	D	H	V

ז	ח	ט	י	כ	כ	ך
Z	CH	T	Y	K	CH	CH

ל	מ	ם	נ	ן	ס	ע
L	M	M	N	N	S	'

פ	פ	ף	צ	ץ	ק	ר
P	F	F	TZ	TZ	K	R

ש	ת	ת
SH	T	T

דָ	וֹ	וּ	וְ	ִ	ְ
ah	eh	oo	oh	ee	-

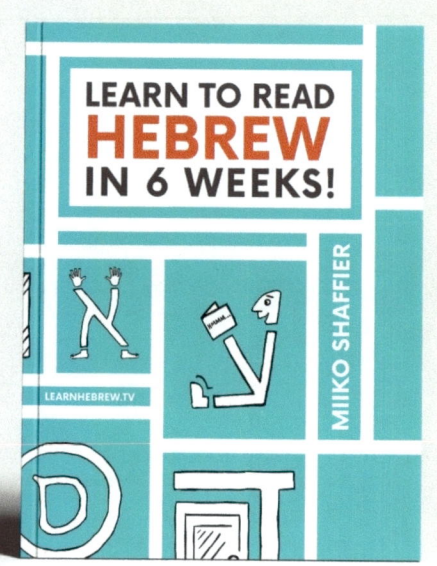